INNOCENCE

&

AWAKENING

POEMS BY DR KV WILT

POINTER OAK

Pointer Oak / Tri S Foundation

© 2016 by Kurt Wilt. All rights reserved

These poems first appeared in the following publications:

Pennsylvania Literary Journal
"Limestone Cliffs Separated"
"Eight, Mark Hacksawed the Rusty Iron Door"

Indian Journal
"I First Remember the Sound"
"Grandma Used to Take Me 'Down Home'"

Bloodstone Review
"Our Wantagh Bows Were Made of Flimsy Sticks"

Primus
"Our First Boat Lay With its Back"
"The Dock Was Twice the Size of Dad's"

First edition. First printing

Edited by Dr Yasmine Van Wilt and Paulette Millichap

Cover art by Denise Daudelin

Book and cover design by Carl Brune

Distributed by Millichap Books
millichapbooks.com

ISBN 978-0-9823274-5-6

Dedicated to Denise, My Beatrice, With Love

I offer my gratitude to Paulette, Millichap Books and the Tri-S Foundation for their belief in and support of my craft. I also wish to thank my dearest friends and family for their unwavering support.

CONTENTS

EDITOR'S NOTE

Innocence and Awakening is comprised of two distinct but interrelated collections of memoire poems. The first collection, *Dante and His Beatrice*, explores the existential crisis of the narrator, poet Dante Alligheri; told from his liminal, omniscient perspective, it is psychically magical real and imagistic. The second collection, *Sonnets*, is composed of sonnets that explore late twentieth century American life. Told from the poet's own perspective, the poems are more quotidian and less imagistic, although still often magical real. Both the first and the second collections focus, thematically, on the narrator-poet's struggle to achieve oneness or wholeness through communion with the higher self; the dialogue, both internal and external, deifies the absent or spectral goddess character placing the narrator in the position of supplicant. Indeed, Wilt positions both romantic and devotional love are vehicles for awakening. These links, informed by Wilt's life-long practice of non-Western meditation, both Sufi and Tibetan Buddhist, and his collaboration with artist-mystic Joseph Rael, are highly indicative of the poet's journey to parallel the sparse, structured discipline of the meditative experience, with both heady and colloquial poetic contemplations.

The work of a mystic and teacher, these exquisite collections reveal the depth of Wilt's consciousness. They are the works of a poet who has lived contemplatively and intuitively, who has devoted himself entirely to the creation of beauty; they are also the manifestation of sincere spiritual and artistic devotion. To me, they are of ilk of the bards with whom Wilt feels affinity: Blake, Rilke, Dante. The muse-poet relationship between Wilt and wife Denise honors a shared lifetime of dedication, both spiritual and artistic. I chose Denise's scarlet oil painting for the cover because I believe it exemplifies the intensity and the power of these poetic works. It also presents, in a powerful visceral form, the importance of the muse-poet relationship. Denise is Kurt's muse; and he is hers.

I believe these collections rank amongst the best of early 21st century Americana and are both deeply moving and rousing; it is my sincere hope that you will enjoy them, as I have. Written over twenty years, Wilt's labor in their creation is evident in their lean, impacting and artful form. It has been my joy to witness their evolution, throughout my childhood and adulthood, and to finally witness their completion and dissemination. Thank you for reading these words; I hope they bear you great joy and comfort.

DR YASMINE VAN WILT

May 2016

PART I

DANTE AND HIS BEATRICE

From the single window
Dante watched
Beatrice walking.
When his watching was one—
pointed, when he witnessed
what Beatrice was,
Death, the night watchman, wore
Dante's shadow. Once
he no longer knew who
he was, Dante witnessed
his love everywhere.

Dante noticed the waves
of the Arno wrestling
the hull of the wooden
ship, reaching for the wheat-
colored thighs of the wife
who abandoned her wash
on the shore while wading,
weeping in the west wind
which lifts the ship's cloth wings,
carrying the ghost
shirt eastward by the wall
where the poet wanders.

Where is Beatrice?
I've awoken trembling
to my own vibration.
Is she walking outside
under the crescent moon
dreaming the same story
about a piece of land
that sings with three voices?
The muse must have woken
her too. I must believe
that Mystery
speaks to us together,
that no matter what
the same lightning strikes us.

Beatrice made him
a poet. A poet abandons
the known to the historians
and hangs upside down
in a wellspring to read
the lustrous lyrics
on the watery wall
behind his eyes.

Beatrice, am I
imagining this?
Am I imagining
you're this amethyst?
Am I imagining
the way the wall, the walk,
the chestnuts, the sunset
borrow your blue? Are you
not the orchestrator
of my gait, my voice, my gasp?
Or am I still the same
boy in love with love,
promising, pretending,
pining for your presence,
painting the landscape
with his own desire?
Or, excavated by you,
am I seeing with the eye
of emptiness, the canvas
onto which all things
expose themselves?
When I was five or six
a Greek sailor gave me
a shell shaped like a fan
whose top was deeply ribbed
with shades of orange and grey
and whose underside was
silver white hues of moon
sloping into a well,

a grotto where my thumb
nestled like a snail.
For weeks I held this
shell in one of my hands
feeling its uncanny
fit, flowing into its
polished interior
or devoutly stumbling
over its rosary
that was sometimes the back
of a leviathan,
sometimes the Apennines.
When I could not hold it
I wrapped it in a scrap
of silk and put it in
my pocket. When I dreamed
I planted it beneath
my pillow like a seed.
I have seen the lost shell
in my man's hands: ridges
in the fingers, tendons,
muscles and bulging veins;
lunar, lily smoothness
in the palms at prayer.
Now my body, rigid,
bowed, stooped at the shoulders,
assumes that shape. Am I
being held? Does someone
hear the sea in me?

Power sends one
person to recognize us,
to sense our six-pointed cross.
This poet was sent to see
the unseen Beatrice.
Love is what Power
feels when the poet's lens
is polished, pushed
inside-out from behind.

Truth is Fact's godfather
and Beauty's maid, what is the
    importance of Beauty over Fact?
the servant who reminds
us the sun is setting
and we're wasting the Power
that mounts with every
incoming wave,
that we're drunk
on cheap wine and can't
find the subtle signs
of our Beatrice.

Beatrice—my malady
and my medicine.
Imagining her
wading in the Arno's
morning mist or filling
amphora at the fountain,
watching stars in midday, I
feel ancestral knots,
Mesozoic reefs rising
in my abdomen. And resist
gripping my shoulders
and knees into a fist.
Then her wind,
that is neither created
nor destroyed, whistles
through the pores, fissures,
and orifices, unbinds
a perfume surge that turns
me inside out.

Beloved muse, you've shown me
that we exist left to right—right to left,
up to down—down to up; time-full
and less; that new pieces exist alone yet
stacked upon—even under—the old.
The saber-eyed madness you've inspired
has conjured long forgotten loves
from the cold dark bottom, from
under the trapdoor in the cellar.
Perhaps old and new are the same;
perhaps today's rain falls in the pool
formed by yesterday's rain; perhaps
today's rain is yesterday's mist.

You arrived with your new face,
a perpetual new moon, hooking
me without bait, guiding me like
Eurydice from behind. When Sirius
dove, you rubbed me with cedar oil,
wound me in linen, buried me in your
back yard with the bulbs. When Sirius
rose, I was a tulip. Gaped upon
by your daughter, who has learned
to walk. Is this is just imagination?
Yes. The flint without which
the brain is but steel.

Screeches keep me awake.
I no longer avoid
through travel, drink, or drug,
the gnawing of small rodents
at my insides.
How did they get in there?
And who put up these walls,
plastered, and painted them?
I'm not consoled by thoughts
of karma or transformation.
Or by the memories
of fallen walls giving way
to savannahs, in spring.
Nor am I dismayed by
freedom—when it finds
itself enclosed in yet
another courtyard
beset by different pests.

You, who are the moonlit
hollow sea within me,
last night I saw a doe
eating beside the road,
the first deer I've seen
in this city. Maybe it
too has been exiled. It
continued to eat grass
as I passed by praying
to be of nature.

Am I invisible?
Have my feet become hooves?
Have my arms sprouted leaves?
Am I a wind-blown spore?
This morning I dreamt I
was sitting cross-legged
on the grass, bent over
on my elbows so my
tapering arms and pressed
fingertips were a temple.
A sparrow flewinto
the sacred space and sang.

Have I become a nest?

Dawn—the sound goes out-down
while the phenomenon appears to rise.
What happened since Orpheus, Adam,
and the Anasazi? When people had
tympanum, when names were what
they heard happening—not words.
Can I notice without naming?
Can I just th-row (fricative openness)
what we call stone in what we call
river and just r-ide what we call
re-ver-ber-a-tions? Never what we call
lunging for a name while it what we call
plunges toward the so-called bottom?

There is no bridge between
mind and intuition,
no missing link between things
and No Thing,
no super-subtle calculation
to imagination,
no super-fast micro-tick from
time to eternity,
no perpetual life span
to immortality.

The peak of the mountain
is just taller.
At no infinitesimal measure
does become sky;
nor does sky ever become
the heaven, the peace
which passeth understanding.

The pathless path to peace
does not pass through repression,
Monks want too little not too much;
they cling to things rather than
No thing. Trying to deny desire,
they smother the fire
that can immolate thought,
strangle the whale
that can swallow self.

To Ravenna spring comes.
Why? Because this city
is nearer to the sun? Why?
This morning fine rain fell.
Why fine? Why rain? Why clouds?
Why fall? Why gravity at all?
Why are we stuck with how
and what? Why do we force
small answers? Do we fear
we'll lose the illusion of control?
Do we fear little why's will lead
to larger and largerones—
till we become One?
Why do we save ourselves
from Awe and Unknowing?

Part of me is weather,
the planetary mood,
the phases of the moon,
the constellation's fool.
But this fluctuating
phantasmagoria
I witness from Sirius,
the hub of the solar system,
the navel from which
all blessings flow.

Desire is the tide
which has been trapped
ashore in shells,
seeming satisfiable.
Till a tsunami tricks it
into sea, where it then clings
to flotsam after flotsam
till, its spark spent,
it slips amid the flames.

The learned are exiled without,
where subjects tame objects;
hence that's all the learned talk about.
Dante was chosen to live within
the well, edgeless and surfaceless,
wherefrom the breath rises as sun,
into which it returns as moon,
out and in, out and in, farther
and further, till without is within.
Now he knows that if one walks
at night, hooded with the lamp
of love, long enough in any direction,
one will be found by the coal-diamond
where-within everything sparks and sputters,
the infinite trick, the slow-quick,
seamless, steaming, bubbling-bursting
stillness where-within planets pirouette,
suns crow and moons drown.
Beatrice, does delirious chit-chat
matter? Can metaphors bear the ken
your senses lent me? I don't care,
Beloved. Drunk on your wine,
I'm just whispering
your name.

The window is open.
I could write that crickets
are angels. But does
it make them any more
a miracle?
I could also write that
listening to their chant
makes my mind a crystal
knife. But what is my mind
without crickets
and what are the crickets
without thought?
Miracles don't need me.
Isn't suchness enough?
How did Earth become profane?
Why the need to compare,
to invoke what we think is up?
Why did someone create
heaven? Couldn't he see?

I am at peace with the
wasps whose milky sponges
surround my house hanging
in perpendiculars.
When I'm sweeping the step,
washing the shutters, or
watering irises
they're hovering around
dangling poison lances
in my face, buzzing near
my ears. Whispering what?
Sometimes they brush my cheek
or crawl among the folds
of my clothing or touch
down in my thin gray hair.
I even talk to them.
What has happened? Five years
ago I was cutting
their umbilical cords,
sweeping them to the street,
afraid they'd sting a child.
Which child? Has the fire
burning haphazardly
inside, the fire I've
struggled to recover,
finally stabilized?
I love red.

When I was a boy, I lay
awake at night, deafened by
the music of the spheres,
mesmerized by the kaleidoscope
of shapes and colors in the space
above my bed.
As a man, I'm the one above,
witnessing events in waking dreams,
from a hill, from a tree, from horseback,
always observing what others do;
never doing.

Such is the outsider,
the perennial traveler,
who studies a land's customs,
who practices rolling consonants
and nasalizing vowels, who forgot
 his mother tongue and mastered
his father tongue—which he stutters.
Is the soul only a spectator?
Is it what is left when
the lion sleeps with the lamb?
Does it have a home?

Fear is a paste joining
the head and feet until
the kingdom comes. Until
the bridegroom breathes
fire into the vigilant
lamps. For vigilant lamps
fear is fuel for conflagration.
When their flames reach sky,
water falls to temper
empty cups, to wet
the garden's scorched dirt,
to pool within the crater
of the soul's volcano.

Heaven's exhalation
is earth's inhalation;
the two, crossing, kiss
and crown each other.
The red king becomes white.
The white queen becomes red.
Their love is consummated
in the pink six-pointed bed
of the heart. The double throne
from which they rule.

Breath is a bridge between
bowls of heaven and Earth
into and out of which life flows.
When breath nests heaven's
bowl, we say it's spirit.
When it sits inEarth's,
we call it matter. When it fills
both, moving up and down
at the same time,
we call it human.

Beatrice, you
found me a brittle leaf
blowing through the bleak
streets of our frozen city.
Entering your doorway,
I was carried to a crag,
perpetually crowned,
contemplating the stars'
icy incandescence,
detesting the dirt glance
of drunken passersby.
I prayed that you would take
the only thing you left:
this pair of grieving eyes.
Instead you sent envoys,
omniscient sentries
who see rubies in rubble.

Beatrice is
a Rosetta stone,
a breathing book,
a wild testament.
What anoints the holy
cannot die, so how can they come
back? Yet those still sealed in
the tomb shout old slogans, hawk old
wine in old skins.

Love is
not a thought, old crows.
Stop modifying behavior.
Pray in the closest. Fast with a smile.
Roll the stone from your eyes.
See Continuum's surprise:
your breath's green
hummingbird kissing
your breast's hyacinth.

To the girl whose father
I am I said, "I must
finish these poems
before I die." She did
not want to hear me speak
of death. So I said,
"The imperative is a wedge—
of geese flying into the wind.
It does not let us choose.
It reveals itself as Death—
the Before, After, and In-
Between. Death, our ally,
inhales time and rides
our left shoulder minding
us of imminent ends
that trigger destiny."

The landscape is a sketch.
I close the linen curtains,
retreating to my cerulean room.
I'm an anchor
plunging inward, a bear
craving hibernation.
Are you the firmament
hiding inside? When I close
my eyelids, the sun, moon,
stars, and planets shine.
But I can't turn my back
on the sketch. I am both
too old and too young
to become an ascetic.
Are you testing me, torturing
me, teaching me, stretching
me? Is this another chapter
of 'being in the world but
not of it'? Are you creating
eyes in the back of my head?

Beatrice, why this thick
sadness today, rising through
me like mist, draping the olive
trees with the cloth of mourning?
The cormorants in my throat
want to plunge in the lake.

Am I feeling one of the family
or me leave the table—for good?
The insulting drunken uncle or
the rosary-praying grandmother
or the grandchild whom she spoons?

Am I feeling you, Beatrice—
when pillars topple on the hill,
when orchards quake and crack,
when steam hisses and seared pears falls
into the fissures? When droplets gather
on the empty branches?

Maybe a new sense has bloomed.

He talks to the wrinkled
body as if it were a beast
of burden, "Old donkey,
just a few more steps up
this rocky hill until
you can refresh yourself
in the spring and sit under
the olive trees."

With wet lips he rests against
an olive trunk and feels
earth and sky mingle along
the spine; four rooks converge
in the branches bringing
news from four directions.
When the sun sets, the poet
rides an elephant down
the Etruscan hill to town.

A noted alchemist,
said to have transmuted ashes
into gold dust, to have known
the Thrice Great Hermes,
cornered Dante in the market.

While Dante caressed
the swollen bellies of eggplant
and admired how purple
spoke green and black,
the arcane doctor preached
how bodily secretions
correspond to the primum mobile.
Nodding respectfully, Dante
reached for the cucumbers.

Habitually braiding
his beard which cascaded
to his waist, the doctor asked,
"Celebrated poet, what wisdom
what wisdom can you share?"
"The cucumbers are pimply."

On the anniversary
of the day your breath stopped
the signora next door
lost another baby,
her fourth, to the fever.
No more lullabies.
No more wailing either.
Is she finally numb?
Has she succumbed to
the ideology
that that side is sweeter,
that her children suffer
no more like the living,
that their souls are free from
their carnal counterparts
to sing everlastingly
with the heavenly host,
that it was willed by some
benevolent deity
that they should agonize
before their mother's eyes?

Will she try again?
Beatrice, how would I survive
the cut that never heals,
the mouth that always cries,
if you weren't inside?

Dante has the man thing
between his legs, but what
is that. A would-be human
must be a lion a against
his inclinations. He must
witness the mousey stirrings
of himself under fallen leaves;
such is the owl part.
Then he must carry
these fragile intimations
like the opossum, then
protect them like the bear.
Last, he must be loyal
to the blueprint of intuition
like the common dog.
Birth is not an arrival
but an invitation.

Wishes arrive like this:
Autumn's phlegm heaps
black maple leaves
on sugar bush.
Emissaries of the arctic
winds arrive, causing
tree sparrows to huddle
on the inner limbs
and draft horses and cattle
to den in the barn.

Maple sap migrates from
the trunk to the deepest roots.
Day afterdarker-shorter-colder
day, snow sifts,sealing
the sugar bush with down.
At the hub of the Earth
on the solstice, a pulsing
begins, a pulsing that will
press itself through capillaries
toward the roots, through
the trunk, to the sky.

New life emerges from
the unknown to the known.
like a splinter.
Like an osprey slices
between indigo and indigo
on its winter way to Africa.
Or the first raindrop
breaks the lake'smirror.

When mind's good/bad collapses,
awareness extends on the sofa,
its liquid breath stretches
from horizon to horizon,
and the protector animals—
lion, wolf, bear, and deer—creep
from the dark forests at the poles
to the moonlit meadow.

For the poet every
thing is a way, every
point is a ray, every
ray is a slice
of all-pervading light—
like this bit of bread,
this Milky Way,
he tosses to the loons:
Attention frames the seen,
isolates awareness
into a cool cylinder.
The beam's blow torch
frees the isness
of the seen, making
amazement in the seer.
Contemplation
transpires in between.

We: a question mark,
an heirloom seed,
a deep-sea treasure chest,
an undecifered text,
an arrow in its quiver,
a charcoal sketch on wet
plaster, a breath left
in the chest, a scarab
sealed in dung.
A species that must become.

Dante, at sixty,
is callow, green,
still undrinkable.
Sitting in hiscellar,
he contemplates
the grapes picked
from the vine, de-
stemmed, trampled
into juice, fermented,
pressed, strained
of their skins,
fermented again,
aged in oak casks
stored in tombs
until ready.

So much energy eddied
in my skull that I walked out,
climbed Etruscan hill, and leaned
my sway back against an elm.
And listened to the wind
section and watched the stars
throb in and out of clouds.

Clouds that unleashed
a summer thunder storm
over the Etruscan stones,
that illuminated
a ragged girl, dressed in dirt,
with long, black matted hair
who crawled from underneath
a rubbish heap. I wondered.
And then I understood.

The ten or twelve-year old
is me, the me girl,
buried under garbage,
surviving off of scraps,
hiding from consciousness.
From the would-be king?
Until the table became
and became round.
I, the table becoming round,
held and welcomed her.

That little girl said
she was surrender,
the grail who had to hide
half-paralyzed while
her muscleless brother
became the myth
and marrow of a man.
While the husband became
a wife, and the grandfather
became a grandmother.
"The nightingale must ride
the shoulders of the ox;
the rabbit must straddle
the back of the
the back of the bear."

Beatrice, were you
the prematurely grey Madonna
in the Chianti-stained apron
whose equine calves tapped
a tarantella on the flagstone,
whose tidal breast caressed
my neck when she stretched
to put a bottle on my table,
who brought me pasta and mussels
without my asking, who perched
on the wine cask like a barred owl,
and peered into my eyes,
unpeeling layer after layer?

When the fog of fear
cleared, three animals appeared:
Thoth, who flew me on its wings
to Thebes; APIS, who pulled
my raft downstream to Heliopolis;
Khepera who led me to Pharos
the index finger of Alexandria.
The graveyard of the house of light.

In its afterglow, I saw its great
submerged stones in the harbor;
Crete on the horns of Minotaur;
the crescent moon cradling Venus:
and Maat, the maiden of death,
whose ostrich feather capped
my head and said in your voice:
"Your cup, though cracked,
has collected the necessary
impressions. Go now to the land
of your birth. Bury yourself
waist deep in the dirt
of your ancestors. Water yourself
with tears until your feet take root.
Unbark your heart to the four
seasons till your tree bears fruit
in the dead of winter.

PART II

THE SONNETS

On Jerusalem Avenue
I still dreamed in Portuguese
till Mom gave me the foot of a blue
coelho. In Terceira hills
one didn't see blue rabbits.
I hung its chain from the front
loop of my Lees and rubbed it
for spelling tests and full counts.
Cuffless, I wore the same jeans
in Bermuda where poison toads
had eaten the rabbits. When
Dad's twelve-foot skiff abandoned
Saint George harbor, a hammerhead
tooth hung from my belt instead.

Our Wantagh bows were flimsy sticks
with knotted cotton string that flipped
twigs toward telephone poles and roofs.
Our St. David bows were bamboo
and our arrows were dry fennel.
In the basement on Mitchell Field
Dad built a crossbow we aimed
at bottle caps and candle flames.
At McGuire we had muscles
enough for recurved fiberglass
bows that we aimed at apples
swinging. And cottontails whose holy
entrails stained our sleeves. Eye became
that at which the arrow aimed.

Our first boat lay with its back
in the sand of Moonlight Bay.
At low tide we braved the slimy
seaweed and Man-O-War to climb
its slippery ribs. The little boys,
as Dad called them, stayed ashore
making sinking rafts of palm fronds,
driftwood, and fishing line they'd found.
While we feigned the skeleton
was the capsized hull of a cabin
cruiser, and the Sergeant Majors
at our toes were the man-eaters
that ate the legs of the pilot
who had ejected a mile out.

Eight, Mark hacksawed the rusty iron door
of the WWII machine-gun bunker.
Hidden in the Castle Harbor hillside.
Umbrellaed by banana trees. In sight
of Kindley's air traffic control tower
where Dad worked the graveyard shift. After
Dad hit the sack, we biked to the barracks,
crept through the patch, dropped down the hatch
into the crypt, ate Oreos, read *Archie* comics
by penlight, gunned Nazi Messerschmitts
and battleships attacking Castle Harbor.
Till I, ten, told the boys who rode motor
bikes. Who wouldn't sneak. Who brought fire. Girls.
And the AP's. Who poured concrete in our portal.

The dock was twice the size of dad's
leaky oblong punt. Was hand-shaped
of concrete, studded with stones and shells.
Stocked with conches and shark skulls.
Surrounded by pink oleanders.
Invisible from the St. David shore.
Found it first when the punt drifted past
Severn Bridge; next when I slit a path
with my hatchet along the bridge
down the decline to the water's edge.
Perfect—the ease of reef aloneness:
wind-glints, encyclopedic-blues, monstrous
shadows, longtails spearing needlefish,
loquat sucking snails, distant whistling ships.

Limestone cliffs separated
the plateau of the multi-purpose
non-denominational base church,
which napped under the enlisted
quarters, from the flight line, sea,
and Base Operations. Grownups going
down to duty drove the slow-sloping
switchback. Kids descending to the beach
and ball fields dared dropping from the back
of the giant clam-sized outcrop, onto
the gangrene iron drain pipe, into
the dark centipede-infested crack
that deposited the kids glad
and gashed on the Bermuda grass.

I was never better.
Dad threw triple twenty after
triple twenty and made every-
thing disappear. Mom was master
of the 40-point Scrabble score
and the curing tale. Mark came closer
to flying and lassoed a wild boar
from his bike. Eric free-dove deeper
into caves and the maw of cancer.
Glenn ran with antlers and strummed "Stairway
to Heaven." I just rode to far away
coves before dawn, wrote on water
with a handline, sang to a lover
I hadn't met, slept by a driftwood fire.

I first remember the sound
in my head when Dad was stationed
at Mitchell. Eight, I slept in the small
room where the stairs met the hall
that telescoped to the bathroom.
First the sound was a high-pitched hum
at night when I lay in bed, my head
to the window and the railroad
tracks. When I listened to the hum, it
swelled, and I saw what I called Planet
Saturn behind my eyes. Its rings spread;
turning purple, blue, green, yellow, red.
The hum has become a chorus;
Saturn a galaxy I call Muse.

First, you must build your fort out
of everyday foot and eye
range—unless it's the crow's nest
of an extraordinarily high
tree, or a hole hidden under
a boulder, or the dank basement
of a haunted, bat-ridden barn.
Wherever, no one can see when
you enter or exit. Next it's
roof and walls should repel rain
and rocks. Then you can bring blankets
and tuna sandwiches to your haven.
Last, you give hints where it's at
and ask someone to attack.

The red socks worn day and night
freshman year demand a rewrite.
Till the untamed memory of ten pair
of rooster red bargain socks reared
its head, the symbol-making brain
had highlighted the thin blue rain
coat the cool junior wore in snow
rather than the thick brown wool coat.
And the blue football gear I picked
over the red when Granma tricked
kid me into choosing my birthday
gift. And at last, after the Navy,
the red and blue Laguna marriage
blanket that still anoints my bed.

Grandma used to take me 'down home'
to West Virginia on the Greyhound.
She had left the farm when Dad was four
for New York where she scrubbed floors.
We always bought mums at the station
for her parents in the Shepherdstown
graveyard. We went to Uncle Hume's
coal mine where he dug black lung.
To Night Hole where WIN tribe kids
sunfished. To Bear Cave where they hid
slaves. To Martinsburg where she taught
me to find dimes on the sidewalk.
Till Grandma, this airman's son saw
up and ahead not back and below.

Nineteen. Sunday morning. New York.
Lying on my bed. On my back.
The aftertaste of beer. Afloat
in January glare. Stared at
by the ceiling's Argos eyes.
Silence storms my skull. Glorifies
its six doors. Quicksilver stillness
waterfalls through the neck, chest,
abdomen, legs, and feet. Empties
every cell. Aside from the tide
of the middle's rise and fall, I
am a Gulf Fritillary—netted, relaxed,
stretched, pinned, and surveyed under glass.

Alone on the Edge of Mt. Lykavitos,
I hear Cole's "I Get a Kick Out of You"
down the hill. I pull back to see you, unlikely
Aphrodite, singing: your black hair pony-
tailed, white scarf, pink T, polka dot calve-
length skirt, shopping bag in each hand, keds.
You grin and ask, "Do you know who I am?
Do you know who you are?" "Je suis une
 poete." You tommy gun my fake French
then decode, "I am the seventh queen
of the universe. Come to my island
tonight." "I can't," I mutter. "Take my hand;
The priest can marry us in the chapel."
I turn to see him lighting candles.

For an Irish ballad
the builder Blair bought
the roofless heartwood box by
the firehouse that had been
Dr. J.T. Bradshaw's birthing
room five teams of blue-black
oxen had drug on balsam
logs up Monastery Bluff
where sisters had built
it as a bathhouse. Blair
adorned the square for us by
adding a long back porch but
the new oblong's tin roof bent
up. Like an open book.

Though many call our one hundred
year-old San Ann cottage tiny
though in thirty years we've added
four rooms, to the otherworldly
island boy it's miraculous.
Unimaginable. So much vaster,
so much dryer, so much safer, so
many less unwanted critters
than the banana-leaved lean-to,
the overturned skiff, the rotten
ocean buoy, the World War II
machine-gun bunker and pup tent.
It even has thangkas, kachinas,
a French accent, and a piano.

We didn't have a cat
but cat after cat had
us, dropped on our doorstep
meowing while we slept
or hanging out, hungry
on the pride's periphery
in the backyard, panting
to be last in the pecking
order for food. Just Precious,
the most timid, is with us.
No longer must she gobble
last the pellets; she wolfs
first before raccoons, worker
ants, toads, and slugs arrive.

We walk a low tightrope, sashay
a zigzagging hide-and-seek path
between Main Street and the wild woods;
between the noon sun and new moon.
Our covenant with green: Cut
with care the flower-shrubs that hug
our cottage. The way you snipped
your hippy locks when they eclipsed
your pupils. The painted veil
is a brackish bay, a fairy tale
where kachinas meet a maiden,
a geezer grows claws, a feral Manx
woos a Giant Lop, a star-nosed mole
munches earthworms on a sundial.

In the locker-room lumber, sag
and hulk of sweaty, middle-aged
men not-quite wrapped in white towels,
I see Dad, Appalchacian hill-
billy, blues-harp playing Quaker,
fighter pilot, husband, father
of four. In the sauna I'm drenched
by squeaking sneakers, the grit-stench
of canvas mats, the crush-careen
of handballs, the thunder-iron
of barbells, the knuckle-scraping thud
of the taller-than-me heavy bag,
of the stick-figure kid miming his
old man's steam-engine intensity.

Looking like a striped long board
the adolescent slug under
the clay pot of clary sage pours
across last night's puddled
condensation like hourglass
sand. Inside, ten feet away, gray
beard, who once upon a time prayed
up the sun from his bear rug, gets
up through a slough of sweat. Singing
the Paiute mind-clearing song, he
manages to wash, pull on painter's jeans,
a red plaid shirt and boots, brew jasmine
chai, grab his beret, scarf, and book bag
before nearly crushing brother slug.

"Instead of 'awesome' why not use
'thunderhead' or 'rhinoceros,'
being-things that impress images
on the right brain, not ideas
on the left brain, for which the reader
must supply image-things in order
to experience. The best make
events that free us from mind: Blake.
'Awesome' does resonate in the bottom-
back of the throat before it blossoms
forth like a peony. However your
poem lacks sound play. And metaphor
and movement: imaginative action. Did
the rhino rumble like a thunderhead"?

The track is cracks and rust
but the train eventually gets
where it intends due
to the tooled attentiveness of its crew
of tricksters—ravens, fox, mule deer,
coyotes, rabbits—who engineer
the iron horse with a perpetual
necklace of health and help
songs they studied over the sweat fires
of Raymond Stone, Paiute fixer.
Who learned them because a Vaudevillian
clown captured the sound-shifting rituals
of Raymond's ghost-dancing uncle
on moldy moon-sized reel-to-reels.

Where Lee found it
Lee's girlfriend, Gloria, my god-
mother, found it in Yod
He Vav He. His father, Martin,
found it in George Fox's log cabin.
Louisa, his future wife, found it
in the flaming hedge of Saint Brigid.
Lee found it when he delivered
the Sunday *New York Herald*
Tribune to Bennie Solomon's
music store on Corona and Junction
where Dvorak's *New World Symphony*
resounded from the gramophone.
Hereon, after his paper route,
Lee worshipped Schubert, Verdi,
andMozart.

On the top cedar shelf
                    in the dark corner
of the sauna, I perch cross-legged. Sing the Ute
mind-clearing song. Till a black beard enters.
Asks, "Sir, can I fill the waterbucket."
Hearing "Sir," sensing his deference,
I become the bleached triangle of driftwood
that holds Bermuda spiral shells, sea fans,
and sea glass above our parents' bed.
When he returns to pour water and sit
three feet from my feet, I am the broken—
winged snowy owl wedged in a slit
on the granite brow of El Capitan.

Before it was a yellow tennis
ball strangling my memory, speech,
and math, it was the drunken tiger
shark with the goatee of our neighbor
who plied the wrecks of Long Island Sound
who picked off young porgy and flounder;
the freckled crew-cut Air Force punk
who scuttled his limey landlord's punt;
the Tunisian pimp who abandoned
me in the Sahara when I said, "Non";
the queen witch whose eyes are middens;
whose twisted mirror targets maidens
whose skulls are full moons and lads
whose abdomens are firebrands.

For the life givers of ICU 216
To me Death has never been danger or an end
but a grey-bearded copper friend,
cover-alled in bark and moss, the singer
of sun and moon songs. And his waterfall-haired lover
in lapis wool robes whose wolf's eyes invite
me to turn my rice paper chest inside
out, to offer all the soft organs, the bone walls, the heat, the
safe corners, the meat, and wine of the hearth.
Knowing them as the most of me, I rip off the paper shell, yell
the original river "Yes" from my rutted antediluvian heels
up and out my star-scarred skull.

"Too bad it's not testicular,
prostrate, or even lung cancer.
Glioblastoma is a bad,
bad actor, that must be treated
aggressively with radiation
and chemo. Though your extraction
was very good, it already sent
out countless spores and filaments
that don't show on an MRI.
Each can become a tumor
if not attacked now. So don't waste
time with a trial. After basic
protocol, you should investigate
all—Vidaza, ABBV, Indoximod,
immunotherapy, Nuvigil,
Trivax, even cannabis oil."

I am the swallow-tailed kite
stitching the mist over last night's
asphalt, the eight-foot indigo snake
in the culvert drivers mistake
for a pipe, the big-eared deer mouse
who's eating Fritos too close
to indigo's snub nose, the poet in
the Camry whose muse shuttles him
to radiation, the tennis ball-
sized tumor blooming in his skull,
the pipestone pipe he carved, the plants
smoldering in the bowl, the chants
they carry from the pulsing ground,
through his hollow stem, up his crown.

www.ingramcontent.com/pod-product-compliance
Lightning Source LLC
Chambersburg PA
CBHW060348050426
42449CB00011B/2870